MW01073407

PHRASEBUUK

— ARABIC —

THE MOST IMPORTANT PHRASES

This phrasebook contains
the most important
phrases and questions
for basic communication
Everything you need
to survive overseas

By Andrey Taranov

T&P BOOKS

Phrasebook + 250-word dictionary

English-Arabic phrasebook & mini dictionary

By Andrey Taranov

The collection of "Everything Will Be Okay" travel phrasebooks published by T&P Books is designed for people traveling abroad for tourism and business. The phrasebooks contain what matters most - the essentials for basic communication. This is an indispensable set of phrases to "survive" while abroad.

You'll also find a mini dictionary with 250 useful words required for everyday communication - the names of months and days of the week, measurements, family members, and more.

T&P Books Publishing
www.tpbooks.com

ISBN: 978-1-78716-924-1

This book is also available in E-book formats.
Please visit www.tpbooks.com or the major online bookstores.

FOREWORD

The collection of "Everything Will Be Okay" travel phrasebooks published by T&P Books is designed for people traveling abroad for tourism and business. The phrasebooks contain what matters most - the essentials for basic communication. This is an indispensable set of phrases to "survive" while abroad.

This phrasebook will help you in most cases where you need to ask something, get directions, find out how much something costs, etc. It can also resolve difficult communication situations where gestures just won't help.

This book contains a lot of phrases that have been grouped according to the most relevant topics. You'll also find a mini dictionary with useful words - numbers, time, calendar, colors...

Take "Everything Will Be Okay" phrasebook with you on the road and you'll have an irreplaceable traveling companion who will help you find your way out of any situation and teach you to not fear speaking with foreigners.

TABLE OF CONTENTS

T&P Books Publishing

PRONUNCIATION

T&P phonetic alphabet	Arabic example	English example
[a]	طَفَى [ṭaffa]	shorter than in ask
[ā]	إختار [iχtār]	calf, palm
[e]	هامبورجر [hamburger]	elm, medal
[i]	زفاف [zifāf]	shorter than in feet
[ī]	أبريل [abrīl]	feet, meter
[u]	كلكتا [kalkutta]	book
[ū]	جاموس [ʒāmūs]	fuel, tuna
[b]	بداية [bidāya]	baby, book
[d]	سعادة [saʿāda]	day, doctor
[ḍ]	وضع [waḍʿ]	[d] pharyngeal
[ʒ]	الأرجنتين [arʒantīn]	forge, pleasure
[ð]	تذكار [tiðkār]	pharyngealized th
[ẓ]	ظهر [ẓahar]	[z] pharyngeal
[f]	خفيف [χafīf]	face, food
[g]	جولف [gūlf]	game, gold
[h]	إتّجاه [ittiʒāh]	home, have
[ḥ]	أحبّ [aḥabb]	[h] pharyngeal
[y]	ذهبيّ [ðahabiy]	yes, New York
[k]	كرسيّ [kursiy]	clock, kiss
[l]	لمح [lamaḥ]	lace, people
[m]	مرصد [marṣad]	magic, milk
[n]	جنوب [ʒanūb]	sang, thing
[p]	كابتشينو [kaputʃīnu]	pencil, private
[q]	وثق [waθiq]	king, club
[r]	روح [rūḥ]	rice, radio
[s]	سخريّة [suχriyya]	city, boss
[ṣ]	معصم [miʿṣam]	[s] pharyngeal
[ʃ]	عشاء [ʿaʃāʾ]	machine, shark
[t]	تنّوب [tannūb]	tourist, trip
[ṭ]	خريطة [χarīṭa]	[t] pharyngeal
[θ]	ماموث [mamūθ]	month, tooth
[v]	فيتنام [vitnām]	very, river
[w]	ودّع [waddaʿ]	vase, winter
[χ]	بخيل [baχīl]	as in Scots 'loch'
[ɣ]	تغدّى [taɣadda]	between [g] and [h]
[z]	ماعز [māʿiz]	zebra, please

T&P phonetic alphabet	Arabic example	English example
['] (ayn)	سبعة [sab'a]	voiced pharyngeal fricative
['] (hamza)	سأل [sa'al]	glottal stop

LIST OF ABBREVIATIONS

Arabic abbreviations

du	-	plural noun (double)
f	-	feminine noun
m	-	masculine noun
pl	-	plural

English abbreviations

ab.	-	about
adj	-	adjective
adv	-	adverb
anim.	-	animate
as adj	-	attributive noun used as adjective
e.g.	-	for example
etc.	-	et cetera
fam.	-	familiar
fem.	-	feminine
form.	-	formal
inanim.	-	inanimate
masc.	-	masculine
math	-	mathematics
mil.	-	military
n	-	noun
pl	-	plural
pron.	-	pronoun
sb	-	somebody
sing.	-	singular
sth	-	something
v aux	-	auxiliary verb
vi	-	intransitive verb
vi, vt	-	intransitive, transitive verb
vt	-	transitive verb

BOOKS

ARABIC
PHRASEBOOK

This section contains
important phrases that may
come in handy in various
real-life situations.
The phrasebook will help
you ask for directions, clarify
a price, buy tickets, and
order food at a restaurant

T&P Books Publishing

PHRASEBOOK
CONTENTS

T&P Books Publishing

Excuse me, ...	ba'd ezznak, ... ،بعد إذنك
Hello.	ahlan أهلا
Thank you.	ʃokran شكراً
Good bye.	ella alliqāʼ إلى اللقاء
Yes.	aywā أيوة
No.	laʼa لأ
I don't know.	maʻrafʃ ما أعرفش
Where? | Where to? | When?	feyn? | lefeyn? | emta? إمتى؟ ا لفين؟ ا فين؟

I need ...	meḥtāg ... ... محتاج
I want ...	ʻāyez ... ... عايز
Do you have ...?	ya tara ʻandak ...? يا ترى عندك... ؟
Is there a ... here?	feyh hena ...? فيه هنا ...؟
May I ...?	momken ...? ممكن ...؟
..., please (polite request)	... men faḍlak ... من فضلك

I'm looking for ...	ana badawwar ʻla ... ... أنا بادور على
restroom	ḥammām حمام
ATM	makīnet ṣarraf ʼāaly ماكينة صراف آلي
pharmacy (drugstore)	ṣaydaliya صيدلية
hospital	mostaʃfa مستشفى
police station	ʼessm el ʃorṭa قسم شرطة
subway	metro el anfāʼ مترو الأنفاق

taxi	taksi
	تاكسي
train station	mahattet el 'attr
	محطة القطر

My name is ...	essmy ...
	إسمي...
What's your name?	essmak eyh?
	اسمك إيه؟
Could you please help me?	te'ddar tesā'dny?
	تقدر تساعدني؟
I've got a problem.	ana 'andy moʃkela
	أنا عندي مشكلة
I don't feel well.	ana ta'bān
	أنا تعبان
Call an ambulance!	otlob 'arabeyet es'āf!
	أطلب عربية إسعاف!
May I make a call?	momken a'mel mokalma telefoniya?
	ممكن أعمل مكالمة تليفونية؟

I'm sorry.	ana 'āssif
	أنا آسف
You're welcome.	el 'afw
	العفو

I, me	ana
	أنا
you (inform.)	enta
	أنت
he	howwa
	هو
she	hiya
	هي
they (masc.)	homm
	هم
they (fem.)	homm
	هم
we	ehna
	احنا
you (pl)	entom
	انتم
you (sg, form.)	haddretak
	حضرتك

ENTRANCE	doxūl
	دخول
EXIT	xorūg
	خروج
OUT OF ORDER	'attlān
	عطلان
CLOSED	moylaq
	مغلق

OPEN	maftūḥ
	مفتوح
FOR WOMEN	lel sayedāt
	للسيدات
FOR MEN	lel regāl
	للرجال

Questions

Where?	feyn? فين؟
Where to?	lefeyn? لفين؟
Where from?	men feyn? من فين؟
Why?	leyh? ليه؟
For what reason?	le'ayī sabab? لأي سبب؟
When?	emta? إمتى؟

How long?	leḥadd emta? لحد إمتى؟
At what time?	fi ayī sā‘a? في أي ساعة؟
How much?	bekām? بكام؟
Do you have ...?	ya tara ‘andak ...? يا ترى عندك ...؟
Where is ...?	feyn ...? فين ...؟

What time is it?	el sā‘a kām? الساعة كام؟
May I make a call?	momken a‘mel mokalma telefoniya? ممكن أعمل مكالمة تليفونية؟
Who's there?	meyn henāk? مين هناك؟
Can I smoke here?	momken addaχen hena? ممكن أدخن هنا؟
May I ...?	momken ...? ممكن ...؟

Needs

I'd like ...	aḥebb ... أحب ...
I don't want ...	meʃ ʿāyiz ... مش عايز ...
I'm thirsty.	ana ʿaṭʃān أنا عطشان
I want to sleep.	ʿāyez anām عايز أنام

I want ...	ʿāyez ... عايز ...
to wash up	atʃaṭṭaf أتشطف
to brush my teeth	aɣsel senāny أغسل سناني
to rest a while	artāḥ ʃwaya أرتاح شوية
to change my clothes	aɣayar hodūmy أغير هدومي

to go back to the hotel	argaʿ lel fondoq أرجع للفندق
to buy ...	ʃerā' ... شراء ...
to go to ...	arūḥ le... ...أروح لـ
to visit ...	azūr ... أزور ...
to meet with ...	a'ābel ... أقابل ...
to make a call	a'mel mokalma telefoniya أعمل مكالمة تليفونية

I'm tired.	ana taʿbān أنا تعبان
We are tired.	eḥna taʿbānīn إحنا تعبانين
I'm cold.	ana bardān أنا بردان
I'm hot.	ana ḥarran أنا حران
I'm OK.	ana kowayes أنا كويس

I need to make a call.

mehtāg a'mel mokalma telefoneya

محتاج أعمل مكالمة تليفونية

I need to go to the restroom.

mehtāg arūh el ḥammam

محتاج أروح الحمام

I have to go.

lāzem amſy

لازم أمشي

I have to go now.

lāzem amſy dellwa'ty

لازم أمشي دلوقتي

Asking for directions

Excuse me, ...	ba'd ezznak, ... بعد إذنك، ...
Where is ...?	feyn ...? فين ...؟
Which way is ...?	meneyn ...? منين ...؟
Could you help me, please?	momken tesā'edny, men faḍlak? ممكن تساعدني، من فضلك؟

I'm looking for ...	ana badawwar 'la ... أنا بادور على ...
I'm looking for the exit.	baddawwar 'la ṭarīq el xorūg بادور على طريق الخروج

I'm going to ...	ana rāyeḥ le... أنا رايح لـ...
Am I going the right way to ...?	ana māʃy fel ṭarīq el ṣaḥh le ...? أنا ماشي في الطريق الصح لـ... ؟

Is it far?	howwa be'īd? هو بعيد؟
Can I get there on foot?	momken awṣal ḥenāk māʃy? ممكن أوصل هناك ماشي؟

Can you show me on the map?	momken tewarrīny 'lal xarīṭa? ممكن توريني على الخريطة؟
Show me where we are right now.	momken tewarrīny eḥna feyn dellwa'ty? ممكن توريني إحنا فين دلوقتي؟

Here	hena هنا
There	henāk هناك
This way	men hena من هنا

Turn right.	oddxol yemīn ادخل يمين
Turn left.	oddxol ʃemal ادخل شمال
first (second, third) turn	awwel (tāny, tālet) ʃāre' أول (تاني، تالت) شارع

to the right

'lal yemīn
على اليمين

to the left

'lal ʃemal
على الشمال

Go straight ahead.

'la ṭūl
على طول

Signs

WELCOME!	marḥaba
	مرحبا
ENTRANCE	doxūl
	دخول
EXIT	xorūg
	خروج

PUSH	eddfaʿ
	إدفع
PULL	ess-ḥab
	إسحب
OPEN	maftūḥ
	مفتوح
CLOSED	moɣlaq
	مغلق

FOR WOMEN	lel sayedāt
	للسيدات
FOR MEN	lel regāl
	للرجال
GENTLEMEN, GENTS (m)	el sāda
	السادة
WOMEN (f)	el sayedāt
	السيدات

DISCOUNTS	taxfīḍāt
	تخفيضات
SALE	okazyōn
	اوكازيون
FREE	maggānan
	مجانا
NEW!	gedīd!
	جديد!
ATTENTION!	ennttabeh!
	إنتبه!

NO VACANCIES	mafīʃ makān
	ما فيش مكان
RESERVED	maḥgūz
	محجوز
ADMINISTRATION	el edāra
	الإدارة
STAFF ONLY	lel ʿāmelīn faqaṭ
	للعاملين فقط

BEWARE OF THE DOG!	ehhtaress men el kalb! إحترس من الكلب!
NO SMOKING!	mammnū' el tadχīn! ممنوع التدخين!
DO NOT TOUCH!	mammnū' el lammss! ممنوع اللمس!
DANGEROUS	χatīr خطير
DANGER	χatar خطر
HIGH VOLTAGE	gohd 'āly جهد عالي
NO SWIMMING!	mammnū' el sebāḥa! ممنوع السباحة!

OUT OF ORDER	'attlān عطلان
FLAMMABLE	qābel lel eʃte'āl قابل للإشتعال
FORBIDDEN	mammnū' ممنوع
NO TRESPASSING!	mammnū' el taχatty! ممنوع التخطي!
WET PAINT	talā' ḥadiis طلاء حديث

CLOSED FOR RENOVATIONS	moχlaq lel tagdedāt مغلق للتجديدات
WORKS AHEAD	aʃγāl fel tarīq أشغال في الطريق
DETOUR	monḥany منحنى

Transportation. General phrases

plane	tayāra طيارة
train	'attr قطر
bus	otobiis اوتوبيس
ferry	safīna سفينة
taxi	taksi تاكسي
car	'arabiya عربية

schedule	gadwal جدول
Where can I see the schedule?	a'dar aʃūf el gadwal feyn? أقدر أشوف الجدول فين؟
workdays (weekdays)	ayām el ossbū' أيام الأسبوع
weekends	nehāyet el osbū' نهاية الأسبوع
holidays	el 'agazāt الأجازات

DEPARTURE	el saffar السفر
ARRIVAL	el wosūl الوصول
DELAYED	mettʾxara متأخرة
CANCELLED	molɣā ملغاه

next (train, etc.)	el gayī الجاي
first	el awwel الأول
last	el 'axīr الأخير

When is the next ...?	emta el ... elly gayī? إللي جاي؟ ... إمتى الـ
When is the first ...?	emta awwel ...? إمتى اول ...؟

When is the last ...?

emta 'āχer ...?
إمتى آخر ...؟

transfer (change of trains, etc.)

tabdīl
تبديل

to make a transfer

abaddel
أبدل

Do I need to make a transfer?

hal ahtāg le tabdīl el...?
هل أحتاج لتبديل الـ...؟

Buying tickets

Where can I buy tickets?	meneyn momken aʃtery tazāker? منين ممكن أشتري تذاكر؟
ticket	tazzkara تذكرة
to buy a ticket	ʃerā' tazāker شراء تذاكر
ticket price	as'ār el tazāker أسعار التذاكر

Where to?	lefeyn? لفين؟
To what station?	le'ayī maḥatta? لأي محطة؟
I need ...	meḥtāg ... محتاج ...
one ticket	tazzkara waḥda تذكرة واحدة
two tickets	tazzkarteyn تذكرتين
three tickets	talat tazāker تلات تذاكر

one-way	zehāb faqaṭṭ ذهاب فقط
round-trip	zehāb we 'awda ذهاب وعودة
first class	daraga ūla درجة أولى
second class	daraga tanya درجة ثانية

today	el naharda النهاردة
tomorrow	bokra بكرة
the day after tomorrow	ba'd bokra بعد بكرة
in the morning	el sobḥ الصبح
in the afternoon	ba'd el zohr بعد الظهر
in the evening	bel leyl بالليل

aisle seat

korsy mammar

كرسي ممر

window seat

korsy ʃebbāk

كرسي شباك

How much?

bekām?

بكام؟

Can I pay by credit card?

momken addfaʿ be kart eʼtemān?

ممكن أدفع بكارت إئتمان؟

Bus

bus	el otobiis
	الأوتوبيس
intercity bus	otobiis beyn el moddon
	أوتوبيس بين المدن
bus stop	maḥaṭṭet el otobiis
	محطة الأوتوبيس
Where's the nearest bus stop?	feyn aqrab maḥaṭṭet otobiis?
	فين أقرب محطة أوتوبيس؟
number (bus ~, etc.)	raqam
	رقم
Which bus do I take to get to ...?	'āχod ayī otobiis le ...?
	أخذ أي اوتوبيس لـ...؟
Does this bus go to ...?	el otobiis da beyrūḥ ...?
	الأوتوبيس دة بيروح ...؟
How frequent are the buses?	el otobiis beyīgi kol 'add eyh?
	الأوتوبيس بيجي كل قد إيه؟
every 15 minutes	kol χamasstāʃar daqīqa
	كل 15 دقيقة
every half hour	kol noṣṣ sā‘a
	كل نص ساعة
every hour	kol sā‘a
	كل ساعة
several times a day	kaza marra fel yome
	كذا مرة في اليوم
... times a day	... marrat fell yome
	مرات في اليوم ...
schedule	gadwal
	جدول
Where can I see the schedule?	a‘dar aʃūf el gadwal feyn?
	أقدر أشوف الجدول فين؟
When is the next bus?	emta el otobīss elly gayī?
	إمتى الأتوبيس إللي جاي؟
When is the first bus?	emta awwel otobiis?
	إمتى أول أوتوبيس؟
When is the last bus?	emta 'āχer otobiis?
	إمتى آخر أوتوبيس؟
stop	maḥaṭṭa
	محطة
next stop	el maḥaṭṭa el gaya
	المحطة الجاية

last stop (terminus)

axer mahatta
آخر محطة (أخر الخط)

Stop here, please.

laww samaht, wa'eff hena
لو سمحت، وقف هنا

Excuse me, this is my stop.

ba'd ezznak, di mahattetti
بعد إذنك، دي محطتي

Train

train	el 'aṭṭr
	القطر
suburban train	'aṭṭr el dawāhy
	قطر الضواحي
long-distance train	'aṭṭr el masāfāt el tawīla
	قطر المسافات الطويلة
train station	mahaṭṭet el 'aṭṭr
	محطة القطر
Excuse me, where is the exit to the platform?	ba'd ezznak, meneyn el ṭarīq lel raṣīf
	بعد إذنك، منين الطريق للرصيف؟

Does this train go to ...?	el 'aṭṭr da beyrūh ...?
	القطر دة بيروح ...؟
next train	el 'aṭṭr el gayī?
	القطر الجاي؟
When is the next train?	emta el 'aṭṭr elly gayī?
	إمتى القطر إللي جاي؟
Where can I see the schedule?	a'dar aʃūf el gadwal feyn?
	أقدر أشوف الجدول فين؟
From which platform?	men ayī raṣīf?
	من أي رصيف؟
When does the train arrive in ...?	emta yewṣal el 'aṭṭr ...?
	إمتى يوصل القطر ... ؟

Please help me.	argūk sā'dny
	ارجوك ساعدني
I'm looking for my seat.	baddawwar 'lal korsy betā'y
	بادور على الكرسي بتاعي
We're looking for our seats.	ehna benndawwar 'la karāsy
	إحنا بندور على كراسي
My seat is taken.	el korsy betā'i maʃɣūl
	الكرسي بتاعي مشغول
Our seats are taken.	karaseyna maʃɣūla
	كراسينا مشغولة

I'm sorry but this is my seat.	'ann ezznak, el korsy da betā'y
	عن إذنك، الكرسي دة بتاعي
Is this seat taken?	el korsy da mahgūz?
	الكرسي دة محجوز؟
May I sit here?	momken a''od hena?
	ممكن أقعد هنا؟

On the train. Dialogue (No ticket)

Ticket, please.
tazāker men faḍlak
تذاكر من فضلك

I don't have a ticket.
ma'andīʃ tazzkara
ما عنديش تذكرة

I lost my ticket.
tazzkarty ḍā'et
تذكرتي ضاعت

I forgot my ticket at home.
nesīt tazkarty fel beyt
نسيت تذكرتي في البيت

You can buy a ticket from me.
momken teʃtery menny tazkara
ممكن تشتري مني تذكرة

You will also have to pay a fine.
lāzem teddfa' ɣarāma kaman
لازم تدفع غرامة كمان

Okay.
tamām
تمام

Where are you going?
enta rāyeh feyn?
إنت رايح فين؟

I'm going to ...
ana rāyeh le...
أنا رايح لـ...

How much? I don't understand.
bekām? ana meʃ fāhem
بكام؟ أنا مش فاهم

Write it down, please.
ektebha laww samaht
إكتبها لو سمحت

Okay. Can I pay with a credit card?
tamām. momken addfa' be kredit kard?
تمام. ممكن أدفع بكريدت كارد؟

Yes, you can.
aywā momken
أيوة ممكن

Here's your receipt.
ettfaḍḍal el īṣāl
أتفضل الإيصال

Sorry about the fine.
'āssef beχeṣūṣ el ɣarāma
آسف بخصوص الغرامة

That's okay. It was my fault.
mafīʃ moʃkela. di ɣaltety
ما فيش مشكلة. دي غلطتي

Enjoy your trip.
esstammte' be reḥlatek
استمتع برحلتك

Taxi

taxi	taksi تاكسي
taxi driver	sawwā' el taksi سواق التاكسي
to catch a taxi	'āxod taksi أخد تاكسي
taxi stand	maw'af taksi موقف تاكسي
Where can I get a taxi?	meneyn āxod taksi? منين أخد تاكسي؟

to call a taxi	an tattlob taksi أن تطلب تاكسي
I need a taxi.	ahtāg taksi أحتاج تاكسي
Right now.	al'āan الآن
What is your address (location)?	ma howa 'ennwānak? ما هو عنوانك؟
My address is ...	'ennwāny fi ... عنواني في ...
Your destination?	ettegāhak? إتجاهك؟
Excuse me, ...	ba'd ezznak, ... بعد إذنك، ...
Are you available?	enta fādy? إنت فاضي؟
How much is it to get to ...?	bekām arūh...? بكام أروح...؟
Do you know where it is?	te'raf hiya feyn? تعرف هي فين؟

Airport, please.	el matār men fadlak المطار من فضلك
Stop here, please.	wa'eff hena, laww samaht وقف هنا، لو سمحت
It's not here.	meʃ hena مش هنا
This is the wrong address.	da 'enwān ɣalat دة عنوان غلط
Turn left.	oddxol ʃemal ادخل شمال
Turn right.	oddxol yemīn ادخل يمين

How much do I owe you?

'layī līk kām?

عليّ لك كام؟

I'd like a receipt, please.

'āyez īṣāl men faḍlak.

عايز إيصال، من فضلك.

Keep the change.

χally el bā'y

خلّي الباقي

Would you please wait for me?

momken tesstannāny laww samaḥt?

ممكن تستنّاني لو سمحت؟

five minutes

χamas daqā'eq

خمس دقائق

ten minutes

'aʃar daqā'eq

عشر دقائق

fifteen minutes

rob' sā'a

ربع ساعة

twenty minutes

telt sā'a

تلت ساعة

half an hour

noṣṣ sā'a

نص ساعة

Hotel

Hello.	ahlan أهلا
My name is ...	essmy ... إسمي ...
I have a reservation.	'andy haggz عندي حجز

I need ...	mehtāg ... محتاج ...
a single room	yorfa moffrada غرفة مفردة
a double room	yorfa mozzdawwaga غرفة مزدوجة
How much is that?	se'raha kām? سعرها كام؟
That's a bit expensive.	di yalya fewaya دي غالية شوية

Do you have anything else?	'andak xayarāt tanya? عندك خيارات تانية؟
I'll take it.	haxod-ha ح أخدها
I'll pay in cash.	haddfa' naqqdy ح أدفع نقدي

I've got a problem.	ana 'andy mofkela أنا عندي مشكلة
My ... is broken.	... maksūr مكسور...
My ... is out of order.	... 'atlān /'atlāna/ /عطلان /عطلانة...
TV	el televizyōn التليفزيون
air conditioner	el takyīf التكييف
tap	el hanafiya (~ 'atlāna) المنفية

shower	el dof الدش
sink	el banyo البانيو
safe	el xāzena (~ 'atlāna) الخازنة

door lock	'effl el bāb
	قفل الباب
electrical outlet	maxrag el kahraba
	مخرج الكهربا
hairdryer	mogaffef el ʃaʕr
	مجفف الشعر

I don't have ...	maʕandīʃ ...
	ما عنديش ...
water	maya
	مية
light	nūr
	نور
electricity	kahraba
	كهربا

Can you give me ...?	momken teddīny ...?
	ممكن تديني ...؟
a towel	fūṭa
	فوطة
a blanket	baṭṭaneya
	بطانية
slippers	ʃebʃeb
	شبشب
a robe	robe
	روب
shampoo	ʃambū
	شامبو
soap	ṣabūn
	صابون

I'd like to change rooms.	ahebb aɣayar el oḍa
	أحب أغير الأوضة
I can't find my key.	meʃ lāʔy meftāḥy
	مش لاقي مفتاحي
Could you open my room, please?	momken tefftaḥ oddty men faḍlak?
	ممكن تفتح أوضتي من فضلك؟
Who's there?	meyn henāk?
	مين هناك؟
Come in!	ettfaḍḍal!
	إتفضل!
Just a minute!	daqīqa wāḥeda!
	دقيقة واحدة!
Not right now, please.	meʃ dellwaʔty men faḍlak
	مش دلوقتي من فضلك

Come to my room, please.	taʕāla oddty laww samaḥt
	تعالى أوضتي لو سمحت
I'd like to order food service.	ʕāyez talab men xeddmet el wagabāt
	عايز طلب من خدمة الوجبات
My room number is ...	raqam oddty howa ...
	رقم أوضتي هو ...

I'm leaving ...	ana māʃy ... أنا ماشي ...
We're leaving ...	eḥna maʃyīn ... إحنا ماشيين ...
right now	dellwaʼty دلوقتي
this afternoon	baʼd el ẓohr بعد الظهر
tonight	el leyla di الليلة دي
tomorrow	bokra بكرة
tomorrow morning	bokra el ṣobh بكرة الصبح
tomorrow evening	bokra bel leyl بكرة بالليل
the day after tomorrow	baʼd bokra بعد بكرة

I'd like to pay.	aḥebb adfaʻ أحب أدفع
Everything was wonderful.	kol ʃeyʼ kan rāʼeʻ كل شيء كان رائع
Where can I get a taxi?	feyn momken alāʼy taksi? فين ممكن ألاقي تاكسي؟
Would you call a taxi for me, please?	momken toṭṭlob lī taksi laww samaḥt? ممكن تطلب لي تاكسي لو سمحت؟

Restaurant

Can I look at the menu, please?

momken aʃuf qã'ema el ṭa'ãm men faḍlak?

ممكن أشوف قائمة الطعام من فضلك؟

Table for one.

tarabeyza le ʃaxṣ wãḥed

ترابيزة لشخص واحد

There are two (three, four) of us.

ehnạ etneyn (talãta, arba'a)

إحنا اتنين (ثلاثة، أربعة)

Smoking

modaxenīn

مدخنين

No smoking

yeyr moddaxenīn

غير مدخنين

Excuse me! (addressing a waiter)

laww samaḥt

لو سمحت

menu

qã'emat el ṭa'ãm

قائمة الطعام

wine list

qã'emat el nebīz

قائمة النبيذ

The menu, please.

el qã'ema, laww samaḥt

القائمة، لو سمحت

Are you ready to order?

mossta'ed toṭṭlob?

مستعد تطلب؟

What will you have?

hatãxod eh?

ح تاخد إيه؟

I'll have …

ana ḥạxod …

أنا ح أخد ...

I'm a vegetarian.

ana nạbãty

أنا نباتي

meat

laḥma

لحم

fish

samakk

سمك

vegetables

xoḍãr

خضار

Do you have vegetarian dishes?

'andak aṭṭbãq nabãtiya?

عندك أطباق نباتية؟

I don't eat pork.

lã 'ãakol el xanzīr

لا أكل الخنزير

He /she/ doesn't eat meat.

howwa /hiya/ la tãkol el laḥm

هو/هي/ لا تأكل اللحم

I am allergic to …	'andy ḥasasseya men … عندي حساسية من …
Would you please bring me …	momken tegīb lī … ممكن تجيب لي…
salt | pepper | sugar	melḥ | felfel | sokkar سكر ا فلفل ا ملح
coffee | tea | dessert	'ahwa | ʃāy | ḥelw حلو ا شاي ا قهوة
water | sparkling | plain	meyāh | ɣaziya | 'adiya عادية ا غازية ا مياه
a spoon | fork | knife	ma'la'a | ʃowka | sekkīna سكينة ا شوكة ا ملعقة
a plate | napkin	ṭabaq | fūṭa فوطة ا طبق

Enjoy your meal!	bel hana wel ʃefa بالهنا والشفا
One more, please.	waḥda kamān laww samaḥt واحدة كمان لو سمحت
It was very delicious.	kanet lazīza geddan كانت لذيذة جدا

check | change | tip	ʃīk | fakka | ba'ʃīʃ بقشيش ا فكة ا شيك
Check, please. (Could I have the check, please?)	momken el ḥesāb laww samaḥt? ممكن الحساب لو سمحت؟
Can I pay by credit card?	momken addfa' be kart e'temān? ممكن أدفع بكارت إئتمان؟
I'm sorry, there's a mistake here.	ana 'āssif, feyh ɣalṭa hena أنا آسف، في غلطة هنا

Shopping

Can I help you?	momken asa'dak? ممكن أساعدك؟
Do you have ...?	ya tara 'andak ...? يا ترى عندك ...؟
I'm looking for ...	ana badawwar 'la ... أنا بادور على ...
I need ...	mehtāg ... محتاج ...
I'm just looking.	ana battfarrag أنا بأتفرج
We're just looking.	ehna benettfarrag إحنا بنتفرج
I'll come back later.	hāgy ba'deyn ح أجي بعدين
We'll come back later.	haneygy ba'deyn ح نيجي بعدين
discounts	sale	taxfīdāt	okazyōn أوكازيون	تخفيضات
Would you please show me ...	momken tewarrīny ... laww samaht? ممكن توريني ... لو سمحت؟
Would you please give me ...	momken teddīny ... laww samaht ممكن تديني ... لو سمحت
Can I try it on?	momken a'īs? ممكن أقيس؟
Excuse me, where's the fitting room?	laww samaht, feyn el brova? لو سمحت، فين البروفا؟
Which color would you like?	'āyez ayī lone? عايز أي لون؟
size	length	maqās	tūl طول	مقاس
How does it fit?	ya tara el maqās mazbūt? يا ترى المقاس مضبوظ؟
How much is it?	bekām? بكام؟
That's too expensive.	da ɣāly geddan دة غالي جدا
I'll take it.	haftereyh ح أشتريه
Excuse me, where do I pay?	ba'd ezznak, addfa' feyn laww samaht? بعد إذنك، أدفع فين لو سمحت؟

Will you pay in cash or credit card?   ḥateddfaʿ naqqdan walla be kart e'temān?
ح تدفع نقدا ولا بكارت إئتمان؟

In cash | with credit card   naqdan | be kart e'temān
بكارت إئتمان ا نقدا

Do you want the receipt?   ʿāyez īṣāl?
عايز إيصال؟

Yes, please.   aywā, men faḍlak
أيوة، من فضلك

No, it's OK.   lā, mafīʃ moʃkela
لا، ما فيش مشكلة

Thank you. Have a nice day!   ʃokran. yome saʿīd
شكرا. يوم سعيد

In town

Excuse me, please.	ba'd ezznak, laww samaḥt
	بعد إذنك، لو سمحت
I'm looking for ...	ana badawwar 'la ...
	أنا بادور على ...
the subway	metro el anfâ'
	مترو الأنفاق
my hotel	el fondo' betâ'i
	الفندق بتاعي
the movie theater	el sinema
	السينما
a taxi stand	maw'af taksi
	موقف تاكسي
an ATM	makînet ṣarraf 'âaly
	ماكينة صراف آلي
a foreign exchange office	maktab ṣarrafa
	مكتب صرافة
an internet café	maqha internet
	مقهى انترنت
... street	ʃâre'...
	... شارع
this place	el makân da
	المكان دة
Do you know where ... is?	hal te'raf feyn ...?
	هل تعرف فين ...؟
Which street is this?	essmu eyh el ʃâre' da?
	اسمه إيه الشارع دة؟
Show me where we are right now.	momken tewarrîny eḥna feyn dellwa'ty?
	ممكن توريني إحنا فين دلوقتي؟
Can I get there on foot?	momken awṣal henâk mâʃy?
	ممكن أوصل هناك ماشي؟
Do you have a map of the city?	'andak χarîta lel madîna?
	عندك خريطة للمدينة؟
How much is a ticket to get in?	bekâm tazkaret el doχûl?
	بكام تذكرة الدخول؟
Can I take pictures here?	momken aṣṣawwar hena?
	ممكن أصور هنا؟
Are you open?	entom fatt-ḥîn?
	إنتم فاتحين؟

When do you open?

emta betefftaḥu?
إمتى بتفتحوا؟

When do you close?

emta beteʾffelu?
إمتى بتقفلوا؟

Money

money	folūss فلوس
cash	naqdy نقدي
paper money	folūss waraqiya فلوس ورقية
loose change	fakka فكة
check | change | tip	ʃīk | fakka | baʔʃīʃ بقشيش فكة شيك
credit card	kart e'temān كارت إئتمان
wallet	maḥfaza محفظة
to buy	ʃerā' شراء
to pay	dafʕ دفع
fine	ɣarāma غرامة
free	maggānan مجانا
Where can I buy ...?	feyn momken aʃtery ...? فين ممكن أشتري ...؟
Is the bank open now?	hal el bank fāteḥ dellwa'ty هل البنك فاتح دلوقتي؟
When does it open?	emta betefftaḥ? إمتى بيفتح؟
When does it close?	emta beye'ffel? إمتى بيقفل؟
How much?	bekām? بكام؟
How much is this?	bekām da? بكام دة؟
That's too expensive.	da ɣāly geddan دة غالي جدا
Excuse me, where do I pay?	ba'd ezznak, addfaʕ feyn laww samaḥt? بعد إذنك، أدفع فين لو سمحت؟
Check, please.	el ḥesāb men faḍlak الحساب من فضلك

Can I pay by credit card?

momken addfa' be kart e'temān?

ممكن أدفع بكارت إئتمان؟

Is there an ATM here?

feyh hena makīnet ṣarraf 'āaly?

فيه هنا ماكينة صراف آلي؟

I'm looking for an ATM.

baddawwar 'la makīnet ṣarraf 'ālly

بادور على ماكينة صراف آلي

I'm looking for a foreign exchange office.

baddawwar 'la maktab ṣarrāfa

بادور على مكتب صرافة

I'd like to change ...

'āyez aγayar ...

عايز أغير ...

What is the exchange rate?

se'r el 'omla kām?

سعر العملة كام؟

Do you need my passport?

enta meḥtāg gawāz safary?

إنت محتاج جواز سفري؟

Time

What time is it?	el sā'a kām?
	الساعة كام؟
When?	emta?
	إمتى؟
At what time?	fi ayī sā'a?
	في أي ساعة؟
now	later	after …	dellwa'ty	ba'deyn	ba'd …
	... بعد ا بعدين ا دلوقتي

one o'clock	el sā'a waḥda
	الساعة واحدة
one fifteen	el sā'a waḥda we rob'
	الساعة واحدة وربع
one thirty	el sā'a waḥda we noṣṣ
	الساعة واحدة ونص
one forty-five	el sā'a etneyn ellā rob'
	الساعة إتنين إلا ربع

one	two	three	waḥda	etneyn	talāta
	تلاتة اتنين ا واحدة
four	five	six	arba'a	xamsa	setta
	ستة اخمسة الأربعة
seven	eight	nine	sabb'a	tamanya	tess'a
	تسعة ا تمانية ا سبعة
ten	eleven	twelve	'aʃra	hedāʃar	etnāʃar
	اتناشر ا حداشر ا عشرة

in …	fi …
	في ...
five minutes	xamas daqā'eq
	خمس دقائق
ten minutes	'aʃar daqā'eq
	عشر دقائق
fifteen minutes	rob' sā'a
	ربع ساعة
twenty minutes	telt sā'a
	تلت ساعة

half an hour	noṣṣ sā'a
	نص ساعة
an hour	sā'a
	ساعة

in the morning	el sobḥ الصبح
early in the morning	el sobḥ badri الصبح بدري
this morning	el naharda el sobḥ النهاردة الصبح
tomorrow morning	bokra el sobḥ بكرة الصبح

in the middle of the day	fi noṣṣ el yome في نص اليوم
in the afternoon	ba'd el zohr بعد الظهر
in the evening	bel leyl بالليل
tonight	el leyla di الليلة دي

at night	bel leyl بالليل
yesterday	emmbāreḥ إمبارح
today	el naharda النهاردة
tomorrow	bokra بكرة
the day after tomorrow	ba'd bokra بعد بكرة

What day is it today?	el naharda eyh fel ayām? النهاردة إيه في الأيام؟
It's ...	el naharda ... النهاردة ...
Monday	el etneyn الإتنين
Tuesday	el talāt التلات
Wednesday	el 'arba' الأربع

Thursday	el xamīs الخميس
Friday	el gumu'ā الجمعة
Saturday	el sabt السبت
Sunday	el ḥadd الحد

Greetings. Introductions

Hello.	ahlan أهلا
Pleased to meet you.	saˈīd be leqāˈak سعيد بلقائك
Me too.	ana assˈad أنا أسعد
I'd like you to meet …	aˈarrafak be … أعرفك بـ ...
Nice to meet you.	forṣa saˈīda فرصة سعيدة

How are you?	ezzayak? إزيك؟
My name is …	esmy … أسمي ...
His name is …	essmu … إسمه ...
Her name is …	essmaha … إسمها ...
What's your name?	essmak eyh? إسمك إيه؟
What's his name?	essmu eyh? إسمه إيه؟
What's her name?	essmaha eyh? إسمها إيه؟

What's your last name?	essm ˈāˈeltak eyh? إسم عائلتك إيه؟
You can call me …	teˈddar tenadīny be… تقدر تناديني بـ....
Where are you from?	enta meneyn? إنت منين؟
I'm from …	ana men … أنا من ...
What do you do for a living?	beteʃtayal eh? بتشتغل إيه؟
Who is this?	meyn da مين دة
Who is he?	meyn howwa? مين هو؟
Who is she?	meyn hiya? مين هي؟
Who are they?	meyn homm? مين هم؟

This is …	da yeb'ā … دة يبقى …
my friend (masc.)	ṣadīqy صديقي
my friend (fem.)	ṣadīqaty صديقتي
my husband	gouzy جوزي
my wife	merāty مراتي
my father	waldy والدي
my mother	waldety والدتي
my brother	aҳūya أخويا
my son	ebny إبني
my daughter	bennty بنتي
This is our son.	da ebnena دة إبننا
This is our daughter.	di benntena دي بنتننا
These are my children.	dole awwlādy دول أولادي
These are our children.	dole awwladna دول أولادنا

Farewells

Good bye!	ella alliqā'
	إلى اللقاء
Bye! (inform.)	salām
	سلام
See you tomorrow.	aʃūfak bokra
	أشوفك بكرة
See you soon.	aʃūfak orayeb
	أشوفك قريب
See you at seven.	aʃūfak el sā'a sab'a
	أشوفك الساعة سبعة
Have fun!	esstammte'!
	إستمتع!
Talk to you later.	netkallem ba'deyn
	نتكلم بعدين
Have a nice weekend.	'ottlet osbū' sa'īda
	عطلة أسبوع سعيدة
Good night.	tessbah 'la xeyr
	تصبح على خير
It's time for me to go.	gā' waqt el zehāb
	جاء وقت الذهاب
I have to go.	lāzem amʃy
	لازم أمشي
I will be right back.	harga' 'la ṭūl
	ح أرجع على طول
It's late.	el waqt mett'axar
	الوقت متأخر
I have to get up early.	lāzem aṣṣ-ha badry
	لازم أصحى بدري
I'm leaving tomorrow.	ana māʃy bokra
	أنا ماشي بكرة
We're leaving tomorrow.	ehhna maʃyīn bokra
	إحنا ماشيين بكرة
Have a nice trip!	rehla sa'īda!
	رحلة سعيدة!
It was nice meeting you.	forṣa sa'īda
	فرصة سعيدة
It was nice talking to you.	sa'eddt bel kalām ma'ak
	سعدت بالكلام معك
Thanks for everything.	ʃokran 'la koll ʃey'
	شكرا على كل شيء

I had a very good time.	ana qaḍḍayt waqt saʿīd
	أنا قضيت وقت سعيد
We had a very good time.	ehna ʾaḍḍeyna waʾt saʿīd
	إحنا قضينا وقت سعيد
It was really great.	kan bel feʾl rāʾeʿ
	كان بالفعل رائع
I'm going to miss you.	hatewwhaʃīny
	ح توحشني
We're going to miss you.	hatewwhaʃna
	ح توحشنا

Good luck!	ḥazz saʿīd!
	!أحظ سعيد
Say hi to …	taḥīāty le…
	…تمياتي لـ

Foreign language

I don't understand.	ana meʃ fāhem
	أنا مش فاهم
Write it down, please.	ektebha laww samaḥt
	إكتبها لو سمحت
Do you speak ...?	enta betettkalem ...?
	انت بتتكلم ...؟

I speak a little bit of ...	ana battkallem ʃewaya ...
	أنا بأتكلم شوية ...
English	engilīzy
	انجليزي
Turkish	torky
	تركي
Arabic	ʻaraby
	عربي
French	faransāwy
	فرنساوي

German	almāny
	ألماني
Italian	iṭāly
	إيطالي
Spanish	asbāny
	أسباني
Portuguese	bortoɣāly
	برتغالي
Chinese	ṣīny
	صيني
Japanese	yabāny
	ياباني

Can you repeat that, please.	momken teʻīd el kalām men faḍlak?
	ممكن تعيد الكلام من فضلك؟
I understand.	ana fāhem
	انا فاهم
I don't understand.	ana meʃ fāhem
	انا مش فاهم
Please speak more slowly.	momken tetkallem abṭaʼ laww samaḥt?
	ممكن تتكلم ابطأ لو سمحت؟

Is that correct? (Am I saying it right?)	keda ṣaḥḥ?
	كدة صح؟
What is this? (What does this mean?)	eh da?
	إيه دة؟

Apologies

Excuse me, please.	ba'd ezznak, laww samaht
	بعد إذنك، لو سمحت
I'm sorry.	ana 'assif
	أنا آسف
I'm really sorry.	ana 'assif beggad
	أنا آسف بجد
Sorry, it's my fault.	ana 'assif, di yalteti
	أنا آسف، دي غلطتي
My mistake.	yaltety
	غلطتي

May I ...?	momken ...?
	ممكن ...؟
Do you mind if I ...?	teddāyi' laww ...?
	تتضايق لو ...؟
It's OK.	mafiʃ moʃkela
	ما فيش مشكلة
It's all right.	kollo tamām
	كله تمام
Don't worry about it.	mate'la'ʃ
	ما تقلقش

Agreement

Yes.	aywā أيوة
Yes, sure.	aywa, akīd ايوة، أكيد
OK (Good!)	tamām تمام
Very well.	kowayīs geddan كويس جدا
Certainly!	bekol ta'kīd! بكل تأكيد!
I agree.	mewāfe' موافق

That's correct.	da ṣaḥīḥ دة صحيح
That's right.	da ṣaḥḥ دة صح
You're right.	kalāmak ṣaḥḥ كلامك صح
I don't mind.	ma'andīʃ māne' ما عنديش مانع
Absolutely right.	ṣaḥḥ tamāman صح تماما

It's possible.	momken ممكن
That's a good idea.	di fekra kewayīsa دي فكرة كويسة
I can't say no.	ma'darʃ a'ūl la' ما أقدرش أقول لأ
I'd be happy to.	bekol sorūr حكون سعيد
With pleasure.	bekol sorūr بكل سرور

Refusal. Expressing doubt

No.	la'a لأ
Certainly not.	akīd la' أكيد لأ
I don't agree.	meʃ mewāfe' مش موافق
I don't think so.	ma 'azzonneʃ keda ما أظنش كدة
It's not true.	da meʃ ṣaḥīḥ دة مش صحيح
You are wrong.	enta ɣalṭān إنت غلطان
I think you are wrong.	azonn ennak ɣalṭān أظن إنك غلطان
I'm not sure.	meʃ akīd مش أكيد
It's impossible.	da mos-taḥīl دة مستحيل
Nothing of the kind (sort)!	mafīʃ ḥāga keda! !ما فيش حاجة كدة
The exact opposite.	el 'akss tamāman العكس تماما
I'm against it.	ana dedd da أنا ضد دة
I don't care.	ma yehemmenīʃ ما يهمنيش
I have no idea.	ma'andīʃ fekra ما عنديش فكرة
I doubt it.	aʃokk fe da أشك في دة
Sorry, I can't.	'āssef ma 'qdarʃ آسف، ما أقدرش
Sorry, I don't want to.	'āssef meʃ 'ayez آسف، مش عايز
Thank you, but I don't need this.	ʃokran, bass ana meʃ meḥtāg loh شكرا، بس أنا مش محتاج له
It's getting late.	el waqt mett'aχar الوقت متأخر

I have to get up early.

lāzem aṣṣ-ḥa badry

لازم أصحى بدري

I don't feel well.

ana ta'bān

أنا تعبان

Expressing gratitude

Thank you.	ʃokran شكراً
Thank you very much.	ʃokran gazīlan شكراً جزيلاً
I really appreciate it.	ana haʾiʾi meʾaddar da أنا حقيقي مقدر دة
I'm really grateful to you.	ana mommtann līk geddan أنا ممتن لك جداً
We are really grateful to you.	eḥna mommtannīn līk geddan إحنا ممتنين لك جداً

Thank you for your time.	ʃokran ʿla waʾtak شكراً على وقتك
Thanks for everything.	ʃokran ʿla koll ʃeyʾ شكراً على كل شيء
Thank you for ...	ʃokran ʿla ... شكراً على ...
your help	mosaʿdetak مساعدتك
a nice time	el waqt الوقت اللطيف

a wonderful meal	wagba rāʾeʿa وجبة رائعة
a pleasant evening	amsiya mommteʿa أمسية ممتعة
a wonderful day	yome rāʾeʿ يوم رائع
an amazing journey	reḥla mod-heʃa رحلة مدهشة

Don't mention it.	lā ʃokr ʿla wāgeb لا شكر على واجب
You are welcome.	el ʿafw العفو
Any time.	ayī waqt أي وقت
My pleasure.	bekol sorūr بكل سرور
Forget it.	ennsa إنسى
Don't worry about it.	mateʾlaʾʃ ما تقلقش

Congratulations. Best wishes

Congratulations!	ohannīk! أهنيك!
Happy birthday!	ʿīd milād saʿīd! عيد ميلاد سعيد!
Merry Christmas!	ʿīd milād saʿīd! عيد ميلاد سعيد!
Happy New Year!	sana gedīda saʿīda! سنة جديدة سعيدة!
Happy Easter!	ʃamm nessīm saʿīd! شم نسيم سعيد!
Happy Hanukkah!	hanūka saʿīda! هانوكا سعيدة!
I'd like to propose a toast.	aḥebb aqtareḥ neʃrab naχab أحب أقترح نشرب نخب
Cheers!	fi seḥḥettak في صحتك
Let's drink to ...!	yalla neʃrab fe ...! يالا نشرب في ...!
To our success!	nagāḥna نجاحنا
To your success!	nagāḥak نجاحك
Good luck!	ḥazz saʿīd! حظ سعيد!
Have a nice day!	nahārak saʿīd! نهارك سعيد!
Have a good holiday!	agāza ṭayeba! أجازة طيبة!
Have a safe journey!	trūḥ bel salāma! تروح بالسلامة!
I hope you get better soon!	atmanna ennak tataʿāfa besorʿa! أتمنى إنك تتعافى بسرعة!

Socializing

Why are you sad?	enta leyh za'lān?
	إنت ليه زعلان؟
Smile! Cheer up!	ebbtassem! farrfeʃ!
	إفرفش! إبتسم!
Are you free tonight?	enta fāḍy el leyla di?
	إنت فاضي الليلة دي؟

May I offer you a drink?	momken a'zemak 'la maʃrūb?
	ممكن أعزمك على مشروب؟
Would you like to dance?	teḥebb torr'oṣṣ?
	تحب ترقص؟
Let's go to the movies.	yalla nerūḥ el sinema
	ياللا نروح السينما

May I invite you to ...?	momken a'zemak 'la ...?
	ممكن أعزمك على ...؟
a restaurant	maṭṭ'am
	مطعم
the movies	el sinema
	السينما
the theater	el masraḥ
	المسرح
go for a walk	tamʃeya
	تمشية

At what time?	fi ayī sā'a?
	في أي ساعة؟
tonight	el leyla di
	الليلة دي
at six	el sā'a setta
	الساعة ستة
at seven	el sā'a sab'a
	الساعة سبعة
at eight	el sā'a tamanya
	الساعة تمانية
at nine	el sā'a tess'a
	الساعة تسعة

Do you like it here?	ya tara 'agbak el makān?
	يا ترى عاجبك المكان؟
Are you here with someone?	enta hena ma' ḥadd?
	إنت هنا مع حد؟
I'm with my friend.	ana ma' ṣadīq
	أنا مع صديق

I'm with my friends.

ana maʿ aṣṣdiqāʾ

أنا مع أصدقاء

No, I'm alone.

lā, ana waḥḥdy

لا، أنا وحدي

Do you have a boyfriend?

hal ʿandak ṣadīq?

هل عندك صديق؟

I have a boyfriend.

ana ʿandy ṣadīq

أنا عندي صديق

Do you have a girlfriend?

hal ʿandak ṣadīqa?

هل عندك صديقة؟

I have a girlfriend.

ana ʿandy ṣadīqa

أنا عندي صديقة

Can I see you again?

aʿdar aʃūfak tāny?

أقدر أشوفك تاني؟

Can I call you?

aʿdar atteṣel bīk?

أقدر أتصل بك؟

Call me. (Give me a call.)

ettaṣṣel bī

إتصل بي

What's your number?

eh raqamek?

إيه رقمك؟

I miss you.

wahaʃtīny

وحشتني

You have a beautiful name.

essmek gamīl

إسمك جميل

I love you.

oḥebbek

أحبك

Will you marry me?

tettgawwezīny?

تتجوزيني؟

You're kidding!

enta bett-hazzar!

إنت بتهزر!

I'm just kidding.

ana bahazzar bas

أنا باهزر بس

Are you serious?

enta bettettkallem gad?

إنت بتتكلم جد؟

I'm serious.

ana gād

أنا جاد

Really?!

ṣaḥīḥ?

صحيح؟

It's unbelievable!

meʃ maʿʿūl!

مش معقول!

I don't believe you.

ana meʃ meṣṣadʿāk

أنا مش مصدقاك

I can't.

maʾdarʃ

ما أقدرش

I don't know.

maʿrafʃ

ما أعرفش

I don't understand you.

meʃ fahmāk

مش فاهماك

Please go away.	men fadlak temʃy
	من فضلك تمشي
Leave me alone!	sebbny lewahhdy!
	اسيبني لوحدي!

I can't stand him.	ana lā atịqo
	أنا لا أطيقه
You are disgusting!	enta mo'reff
	إنت مقرف
I'll call the police!	haṭṭlob el ʃorta
	ح أطلب الشرطة

Sharing impressions. Emotions

I like it.	ye'gebny يعجبني
Very nice.	laṭīf geddan لطيف جدا
That's great!	da rā'e' دة رائع
It's not bad.	da meʃ saye' دة مش سيء
I don't like it.	meʃ 'agebny مش عاجبني
It's not good.	meʃ kowayīs مش كويس
It's bad.	da saye' دة سيء
It's very bad.	da saye' geddan دة سيء جدا
It's disgusting.	da mo'rreff دة مقرف
I'm happy.	ana saʿīd أنا سعيد
I'm content.	ana mabsūṭ أنا مبسوط
I'm in love.	ana baḥebb أنا باحب
I'm calm.	ana hāḍy أنا هادي
I'm bored.	ana zaḥ'ān أنا زهقان
I'm tired.	ana ta'bān أنا تعبان
I'm sad.	ana ḥazīn أنا حزين
I'm frightened.	ana xāyef أنا خايف
I'm angry.	ana ɣadbān أنا غضبان
I'm worried.	ana qalqān أنا قلقان
I'm nervous.	ana mutawwatter أنا متوتر

I'm jealous. (envious)	ana ɣayrān أنا غيران
I'm surprised.	ana mutafāge' أنا متفاجئ
I'm perplexed.	ana morrtabek أنا مرتبك

Problems. Accidents

I've got a problem.	ana 'andy moʃkela أنا عندي مشكلة
We've got a problem.	ehna 'andena moʃkela إحنا عندنا مشكلة
I'm lost.	ana tāʒeh أنا تايه
I missed the last bus (train).	fātny 'āaχer otobiis فاتني آخر أوتوبيس
I don't have any money left.	meʃ fādel ma'aya flūss مش فاضل معايا فلوس
I've lost my ...	dā' menny ... betā'y ضاع مني ... بتاعي
Someone stole my ...	hadd sara' ... betā'y حد سرق ... بتاعي
passport	bassbore باسبور
wallet	mahfaza محفظة
papers	awwarā' أوراق
ticket	tazzkara تذكرة
money	folūss فلوس
handbag	ʃannṭa شنطة
camera	kamera كاميرا
laptop	lab tob لاب توب
tablet computer	tablet تابلت
mobile phone	telefon mahmūl تليفون محمول
Help me!	sā'dny! ساعدني!
What's happened?	eh elly haṣal? إيه إللي حصل؟
fire	harīqa حريقة

shooting	ḍarrb nār
	ضرب نار
murder	qattl
	قتل
explosion	ennfegār
	إنفجار
fight	xenā'a
	خناقة

Call the police!	ettaṣel bel ʃorṭa!
	اتصل بالشرطة!
Please hurry up!	besor'a men faḍlak!
	بسرعة من فضلك!
I'm looking for the police station.	baddawwar 'la qessm el ʃorṭa
	بادور على قسم الشرطة
I need to make a call.	meḥtāg a'mel mokalma telefoneya
	محتاج أعمل مكالمة تليفونية
May I use your phone?	momken asstaxdem telefonak?
	ممكن أستخدم تليفونك؟

I've been …	ana kont …
	أنا كنت ...
mugged	ettnaʃalt
	اتنشلت
robbed	ettsaraqt
	اتسرقت
raped	oɣtiṣabt
	اغتصبت
attacked (beaten up)	ta'arraḍt le e'tedā'
	تعرضت لإعتداء

Are you all right?	enta bexeyr?
	إنت بخير؟
Did you see who it was?	ya tara ʃoft meyn?
	يا ترى شفت مين؟
Would you be able to recognize the person?	te'ddar tett'arraf 'la el ʃaxṣ da?
	تقدر تتعرف على الشخص دة؟
Are you sure?	enta muta'kked?
	إنت متأكد؟

Please calm down.	argūk ehda
	أرجوك إهدا
Take it easy!	hawwen 'aleyk!
	هون عليك!
Don't worry!	mate'la'ʃ!
	أما تقلقش!
Everything will be fine.	kol ʃey' ḥaykūn tamām
	كل شيء ح يكون تمام
Everything's all right.	kol ʃey' tamām
	كل شيء تمام
Come here, please.	ta'āla hena laww samaḥt
	تعالى هنا لو سمحت

I have some questions for you.

'andy līk as'ela

عندي لك أسئلة

Wait a moment, please.

esstanna laḥza men faḍlak

إستنى لحظة من فضلك

Do you have any I.D.?

'andak raqam qawwmy

عندك رقم قومي

Thanks. You can leave now.

ʃokran. momken temʃy dellwa'ty

شكراً. ممكن تمشي دلوقتي

Hands behind your head!

eydeyk wara rāsak!

!إيديك ورا راسك

You're under arrest!

enta maqbūḍ 'aleyk!

!إنت مقبوض عليك

Health problems

Please help me.	argūk sā'dny
	أرجوك ساعدني
I don't feel well.	ana ta'bān
	أنا تعبان
My husband doesn't feel well.	gouzy ta'bān
	جوزي تعبان
My son ...	ebny ...
	إبني ...
My father ...	waldy ...
	والدي ...

My wife doesn't feel well.	merāty ta'bāna
	مراتي تعابة
My daughter ...	bennty ...
	بنتي ...
My mother ...	waldety ...
	والدتي ...

I've got a ...	ana 'andy ...
	أنا عندي ...
headache	ṣodā'
	صداع
sore throat	eḥtiqān fel zore
	إحتقان في الزور
stomach ache	mayaṣṣ
	مغص
toothache	alam aṣnān
	ألم أسنان

I feel dizzy.	ʃā'er be dawār
	شاعر بدوار
He has a fever.	'andak homma
	عنده حمي
She has a fever.	'andaha homma
	عندها حمي
I can't breathe.	meʃ 'āder attnaffess
	مش قادر أتنفس

I'm short of breath.	meʃ 'āder attnaffess
	مش قادر أتنفس
I am asthmatic.	ana 'andy azzma
	أنا عندي أزمة
I am diabetic.	ana 'andy el sokkar
	أنا عندي السكر

I can't sleep.

mef 'āder anām

مش قادر أنام

food poisoning

tassammom γezā'y

تسمم غذائي

It hurts here.

betewwga' hena

بتوجع هنا

Help me!

sā'edny!

ساعدني!

I am here!

ana hena!

أنا هنا!

We are here!

ehna hena!

إحنا هنا!

Get me out of here!

xarragūny men hena

خرجوني من هنا

I need a doctor.

ana mehtāg tabīb

أنا محتاج طبيب

I can't move.

mef 'āder at-harrak

مش قادر أتحرك

I can't move my legs.

mef 'āder aharrak reglaya

مش قادر أحرك رجلية

I have a wound.

'andy garrhh

عندي جرح

Is it serious?

da beggad?

دة بجد؟

My documents are in my pocket.

awwrā'y fi geyby

أوراقي في جيبي

Calm down!

ehhda'!

إهدا!

May I use your phone?

momken asstaxdem telefonak?

ممكن أستخدم تليفونك؟

Call an ambulance!

otlob 'arabeyet es'āf!

أطلب عربية إسعاف!

It's urgent!

di hāla messta'gela!

دي حالة مستعجلة!

It's an emergency!

di hāla tāre'a!

دي حالة طارئة!

Please hurry up!

besor'a men fadlak!

بسرعة من فضلك!

Would you please call a doctor?

momken tekallem doktore men fadlak?

ممكن تكلم دكتور من فضلك؟

Where is the hospital?

feyn el mostaffa?

فين المستشفى؟

How are you feeling?

hāsses be eyh dellwa'ty

حاسس بإيه دلوقتي؟

Are you all right?

enta bexeyr?

إنت بخير؟

What's happened?

eh elly hasal?

إيه إللي حصل؟

I feel better now.

ana ḥāsseṣ eny aḥssan dellwa'ty

أنا حاسس إني أحسن دلوقتي

It's OK.

tamām

تمام

It's all right.

kollo tamām

كله تمام

At the pharmacy

pharmacy (drugstore)	ṣaydaliya
	صيدلية
24-hour pharmacy	ṣaydaliya arbʿa we ʿeʃrīn sāʿa
	صيدلية 24 ساعة
Where is the closest pharmacy?	feyn aqrab ṣaydaliya?
	فين أقرب صيدلية؟

Is it open now?	hiya fat-ḥa dellwaʾty?
	هي فاتحة دلوقتي؟
At what time does it open?	betefftaḥ emta?
	بتفتح إمتى؟
At what time does it close?	beteʾffel emta?
	بتقفل إمتى؟

Is it far?	hiya beʿeyda?
	هي بعيدة؟
Can I get there on foot?	momken awṣal henāk māʃy?
	ممكن أوصل هناك ماشي؟
Can you show me on the map?	momken tewarrīny ʿal xarīṭa?
	ممكن توريني على الخريطة؟

Please give me something for ...	men fadlak eddīny ḥāga le...
	من فضلك إديني حاجة لـ...
a headache	el sodāʿ
	الصداع
a cough	el kohha
	الكحة
a cold	el bard
	البرد
the flu	influenza
	الأنفلوانزا

a fever	el ḥumma
	الحمى
a stomach ache	el mayaṣṣ
	المغص
nausea	el ɣasayān
	الغثيان
diarrhea	el es-hāl
	الإسهال
constipation	el emsāk
	الإمساك
pain in the back	alam fel ẓahr
	ألم في الظهر

chest pain	alam fel ṣadr
	ألم في الصدر
side stitch	γorrza ganebiya
	غرزة جانبية
abdominal pain	alam fel baṭṭn
	ألم في البطن

pill	ḥabba
	حبة
ointment, cream	marham, krīm
	مرهم، كريم
syrup	ʃarāb
	شراب
spray	baxāx
	بخاخ
drops	noqaṭṭ
	نقط

You need to go to the hospital.	enta meḥtāg terūh
	انت محتاج تروح المستشفى
health insurance	taʾmīn ṣeḥhy
	تأمين صحي
prescription	roʃetta
	روشتة
insect repellant	ṭāred lel haʃarāt
	طارد للحشرات
Band Aid	blastar
	بلاستر

The bare minimum

Excuse me, ...	ba'd ezznak, ... بعد إذنك، ...
Hello.	ahlan أهلا
Thank you.	ʃokran شكرا
Good bye.	ella alliqāʾ إلى اللقاء
Yes.	aywā أيوة
No.	laʾa لأ
I don't know.	maʿrafʃ ما أعرفش
Where? | Where to? | When?	feyn? | lefeyn? | emta? إمتى؟ | لفين؟ | فين؟

I need ...	mehtāg ... محتاج ...
I want ...	ʿāyez ... عايز ...
Do you have ...?	ya tara ʿandak ...? يا ترى عندك... ؟
Is there a ... here?	feyh hena ...? فيه هنا ...؟
May I ...?	momken ...? ممكن ...؟
..., please (polite request)	... men faḍlak من فضلك ...

I'm looking for ...	ana badawwar ʿla ... أنا بادور على ...
restroom	ḥammām حمام
ATM	makīnet ṣarraf ʾāaly ماكينة صراف آلي
pharmacy (drugstore)	ṣaydaliya صيدلية
hospital	mostaʃfa مستشفى
police station	ʾessm el ʃorṭa قسم شرطة
subway	metro el anfāʾ مترو الأنفاق

taxi	taksi تاكسي
train station	mahattet el 'attr محطة القطر

My name is ...	essmy ... إسمي...
What's your name?	essmak eyh? اسمك إيه؟
Could you please help me?	te'ddar tesā'dny? تقدر تساعدني؟
I've got a problem.	ana 'andy moʃkela أنا عندي مشكلة
I don't feel well.	ana ta'bān أنا تعبان
Call an ambulance!	otlob 'arabeyet es'āf! اطلب عربية إسعاف!
May I make a call?	momken a'mel mokalma telefoniya? ممكن أعمل مكالمة تليفونية؟

I'm sorry.	ana 'āssif أنا آسف
You're welcome.	el 'afw العفو

I, me	ana أنا
you (inform.)	enta أنت
he	howwa هو
she	hiya هي
they (masc.)	homm هم
they (fem.)	homm هم
we	ehna احنا
you (pl)	entom انتم
you (sg, form.)	haddretak حضرتك

ENTRANCE	doxūl دخول
EXIT	xorūg خروج
OUT OF ORDER	'attlān عطلان
CLOSED	moxlaq مغلق

OPEN	maftūḥ
	مفتوح
FOR WOMEN	lel sayedāt
	للسيدات
FOR MEN	lel regāl
	للرجال

MINI DICTIONARY

This section contains 250 useful words required for everyday communication. You will find the names of months and days of the week here. The dictionary also contains topics such as colors, measurements, family, and more

DICTIONARY CONTENTS

T&P Books Publishing

1. Time. Calendar

time	waqt (m)	وقت
hour	sā'a (f)	ساعة
half an hour	niṣf sā'a (m)	نصف ساعة
minute	daqīqa (f)	دقيقة
second	θāniya (f)	ثانية
today (adv)	al yawm	اليوم
tomorrow (adv)	ɣadan	غدًا
yesterday (adv)	ams	أمس
Monday	yawm al iθnayn (m)	يوم الإثنين
Tuesday	yawm aθ θulāθā' (m)	يوم الثلاثاء
Wednesday	yawm al arbi'ā' (m)	يوم الأربعاء
Thursday	yawm al χamīs (m)	يوم الخميس
Friday	yawm al ʒum'a (m)	يوم الجمعة
Saturday	yawm as sabt (m)	يوم السبت
Sunday	yawm al aḥad (m)	يوم الأحد
day	yawm (m)	يوم
working day	yawm 'amal (m)	يوم عمل
public holiday	yawm al 'uṭla ar rasmiyya (m)	يوم العطلة الرسمية
weekend	ayyām al 'uṭla (pl)	أيام العطلة
week	usbū' (m)	أسبوع
last week (adv)	fil isbū' al māḍi	في الأسبوع الماضي
next week (adv)	fil isbū' al qādim	في الأسبوع القادم
in the morning	fiṣ ṣabāḥ	في الصباح
in the afternoon	ba'd aẓ ẓuhr	بعد الظهر
in the evening	fil masā'	في المساء
tonight (this evening)	al yawm fil masā'	اليوم في المساء
at night	bil layl	بالليل
midnight	muntaṣif al layl (m)	منتصف الليل
January	yanāyir (m)	يناير
February	fibrāyir (m)	فبراير
March	māris (m)	مارس
April	abrīl (m)	أبريل
May	māyu (m)	مايو
June	yūnyu (m)	يونيو
July	yūlyu (m)	يوليو
August	aɣusṭus (m)	أغسطس

September	sibtambar (m)	سبتمبر
October	uktūbir (m)	أكتوبر
November	nuvimbar (m)	نوفمبر
December	disimbar (m)	ديسمبر

in spring	fir rabī‘	في الربيع
in summer	fiṣ ṣayf	في الصيف
in fall	fil χarīf	في الخريف
in winter	fiʃ ʃitā’	في الشتاء

month	ʃahr (m)	شهر
season (summer, etc.)	faṣl (m)	فصل
year	sana (f)	سنة

2. Numbers. Numerals

0 zero	ṣifr	صفر
1 one	wāḥid	واحد
2 two	iθnān	إثنان
3 three	θalāθa	ثلاثة
4 four	arba‘a	أربعة

5 five	χamsa	خمسة
6 six	sitta	ستّة
7 seven	sab‘a	سبعة
8 eight	θamāniya	ثمانية
9 nine	tis‘a	تسعة
10 ten	‘aʃara	عشرة

11 eleven	aḥad ‘aʃar	أحد عشر
12 twelve	iθnā ‘aʃar	إثنا عشر
13 thirteen	θalāθat ‘aʃar	ثلاثة عشر
14 fourteen	arba‘at ‘aʃar	أربعة عشر
15 fifteen	χamsat ‘aʃar	خمسة عشر

16 sixteen	sittat ‘aʃar	ستّة عشر
17 seventeen	sab‘at ‘aʃar	سبعة عشر
18 eighteen	θamāniyat ‘aʃar	ثمانية عشر
19 nineteen	tis‘at ‘aʃar	تسعة عشر

20 twenty	‘iʃrūn	عشرون
30 thirty	θalāθīn	ثلاثون
40 forty	arba‘ūn	أربعون
50 fifty	χamsūn	خمسون

60 sixty	sittūn	ستّون
70 seventy	sab‘ūn	سبعون
80 eighty	θamānūn	ثمانون
90 ninety	tis‘ūn	تسعون
100 one hundred	mi’a	مائة

200 two hundred	mi'atān	مائتان
300 three hundred	θalāθumi'a	ثلاثمائة
400 four hundred	rub'umi'a	أربعمائة
500 five hundred	χamsumi'a	خمسمائة
600 six hundred	sittumi'a	ستّمائة
700 seven hundred	sab'umi'a	سبعمائة
800 eight hundred	θamānimi'a	ثمانمائة
900 nine hundred	tis'umi'a	تسعمائة
1000 one thousand	alf	ألف
10000 ten thousand	'aʃarat 'ālāf	عشرة آلاف
one hundred thousand	mi'at alf	مائة ألف
million	milyūn (m)	مليون
billion	milyār (m)	مليار

3. Humans. Family

man (adult male)	raʒul (m)	رجل
young man	ʃābb (m)	شابّ
woman	imra'a (f)	إمرأة
girl (young woman)	fatāt (f)	فتاة
old man	'aʒūz (m)	عجوز
old woman	'aʒūza (f)	عجوزة
mother	umm (f)	أمّ
father	ab (m)	أب
son	ibn (m)	إبن
daughter	ibna (f)	إبنة
brother	aχ (m)	أخ
sister	uχt (f)	أخت
parents	wālidān (du)	والدان
child	ṭifl (m)	طفل
children	aṭfāl (pl)	أطفال
stepmother	zawʒat al ab (f)	زوجة الأب
stepfather	zawʒ al umm (m)	زوج الأمّ
grandmother	ʒidda (f)	جدّة
grandfather	ʒadd (m)	جدّ
grandson	ḥafīd (m)	حفيد
granddaughter	ḥafīda (f)	حفيدة
grandchildren	aḥfād (pl)	أحفاد
uncle	'amm (m), χāl (m)	عمّ، خال
aunt	'amma (f), χāla (f)	عمّة، خالة
nephew	ibn al aχ (m), ibn al uχt (m)	إبن الأخ، إبن الأخت
niece	ibnat al aχ (f), ibnat al uχt (f)	إبنة الأخ، إبنة الأخت
wife	zawʒa (f)	زوجة

husband	zawʒ (m)	زوج
married (masc.)	mutazawwiʒ	متزوج
married (fem.)	mutazawwiʒa	متزوجة
widow	armala (f)	أرملة
widower	armal (m)	أرمل

| name (first name) | ism (m) | إسم |
| surname (last name) | ism al 'ā'ila (m) | إسم العائلة |

relative	qarīb (m)	قريب
friend (masc.)	ṣadīq (m)	صديق
friendship	ṣadāqa (f)	صداقة

partner	rafīq (m)	رفيق
superior (n)	ra'īs (m)	رئيس
colleague	zamīl (m)	زميل
neighbors	ʒirān (pl)	جيران

4. Human body

body	ʒism (m)	جسم
heart	qalb (m)	قلب
blood	dam (m)	دم
brain	muχχ (m)	مخ

bone	'aẓm (m)	عظم
spine (backbone)	'amūd faqriy (m)	عمود فقريّ
rib	ḍil' (m)	ضلع
lungs	ri'atān (du)	رئتان
skin	buʃra (m)	بشرة

head	ra's (m)	رأس
face	waʒh (m)	وجه
nose	anf (m)	أنف
forehead	ʒabha (f)	جبهة
cheek	χadd (m)	خدّ

mouth	fam (m)	فم
tongue	lisān (m)	لسان
tooth	sinn (f)	سنّ
lips	ʃifāh (pl)	شفاه
chin	ðaqan (m)	ذقن

ear	uðun (f)	أذن
neck	raqaba (f)	رقبة
eye	'ayn (f)	عين
pupil	ḥadaqa (f)	حدقة
eyebrow	ḥāʒib (m)	حاجب
eyelash	rimʃ (m)	رمش
hair	ʃa'r (m)	شعر

hairstyle	tasrīḥa (f)	تسريحة
mustache	ʃawārib (pl)	شوارب
beard	liḥya (f)	لحية
to have (a beard, etc.)	'indahu	عنده
bald (adj)	aṣla'	أصلع

hand	yad (m)	يد
arm	ðirā' (f)	ذراع
finger	iṣba' (m)	إصبع
nail	ẓufr (m)	ظفر
palm	kaff (f)	كفّ

shoulder	katf (f)	كتف
leg	riʒl (f)	رجل
knee	rukba (f)	ركبة
heel	'aqb (m)	عقب
back	ẓahr (m)	ظهر

5. Clothing. Personal accessories

clothes	malābis (pl)	ملابس
coat (overcoat)	mi'ṭaf (m)	معطف
fur coat	mi'ṭaf farw (m)	معطف فرو
jacket (e.g., leather ~)	ʒākīt (m)	جاكيت
raincoat (trenchcoat, etc.)	mi'ṭaf lil maṭar (m)	معطف للمطر

shirt (button shirt)	qamīṣ (m)	قميص
pants	banṭalūn (m)	بنطلون
suit jacket	sutra (f)	سترة
suit	badla (f)	بدلة

dress (frock)	fustān (m)	فستان
skirt	tannūra (f)	تنّورة
T-shirt	ti ʃirt (m)	تي شيرت
bathrobe	θawb ḥammām (m)	ثوب حمّام
pajamas	biʒāma (f)	بيجاما
workwear	θiyāb al 'amal (m)	ثياب العمل

underwear	malābis dāxiliyya (pl)	ملابس داخليّة
socks	ʒawārib (pl)	جوارب
bra	ḥammālat ṣadr (f)	حمّالة صدر
pantyhose	ʒawārib kulūn (pl)	جوارب كولون
stockings (thigh highs)	ʒawārib nisā'iyya (pl)	جوارب نسائية
bathing suit	libās sibāḥa (m)	لباس سباحة

hat	qubba'a (f)	قبّعة
footwear	aḥðiya (pl)	أحذية
boots (e.g., cowboy ~)	būt (m)	بوت
heel	ka'b (m)	كعب
shoestring	ʃarīṭ (m)	شريط

shoe polish	warnīʃ al ḥiðāʾ (m)	ورنيش الحذاء
gloves	quffāz (m)	قفّاز
mittens	quffāz muɣlaq (m)	قفّاز مغلق
scarf (muffler)	ʃʃārb (m)	إيشارب
glasses (eyeglasses)	naẓẓāra (f)	نظّارة
umbrella	ʃamsiyya (f)	شمسيّة

tie (necktie)	karavatta (f)	كرافتة
handkerchief	mandīl (m)	منديل
comb	miʃṭ (m)	مشط
hairbrush	furʃat ʃaʿr (f)	فرشة شعر

buckle	bukla (f)	بكلة
belt	ḥizām (m)	حزام
purse	ʃanṭat yad (f)	شنطة يد

6. House. Apartment

apartment	ʃaqqa (f)	شقّة
room	ɣurfa (f)	غرفة
bedroom	ɣurfat an nawm (f)	غرفة النوم
dining room	ɣurfat il akl (f)	غرفة الأكل

living room	ṣālat al istiqbāl (f)	صالة الإستقبال
study (home office)	maktab (m)	مكتب
entry room	madɣal (m)	مدخل
bathroom (room with a bath or shower)	ḥammām (m)	حمّام
half bath	ḥammām (m)	حمّام

vacuum cleaner	miknasa kahrabāʾiyya (f)	مكنسة كهربائيّة
mop	mimsaḥa ṭawīla (f)	ممسحة طويلة
dust cloth	mimsaḥa (f)	ممسحة
short broom	miqaʃʃa (f)	مقشّة
dustpan	ʒārūf (m)	جاروف

furniture	aθāθ (m)	أثاث
table	maktab (m)	مكتب
chair	kursiy (m)	كرسيّ
armchair	kursiy (m)	كرسيّ

mirror	mirʾāt (f)	مرآة
carpet	siʒāda (f)	سجادة
fireplace	midfaʾa ḥāʾiṭiyya (f)	مدفأة حائطيّة
drapes	satāʾir (pl)	ستائر
table lamp	misbāḥ aṭ ṭāwila (m)	مصباح الطاولة
chandelier	naʒafa (f)	نجفة

kitchen	maṭbaχ (m)	مطبخ
gas stove (range)	butuɣāz (m)	بوتوغاز

electric stove	furn kaharabā'iy (m)	فرن كهربائيّ
microwave oven	furn al mikruwayv (m)	فرن الميكروويف
refrigerator	θallāʒa (f)	ثلاجة
freezer	frīzir (m)	فريزير
dishwasher	ɣassāla (f)	غسّالة
faucet	ḥanafiyya (f)	حنفيّة
meat grinder	farrāmat laḥm (f)	فرّامة لحم
juicer	ʿaṣṣāra (f)	عصّارة
toaster	maḥmaṣat xubz (f)	محمصة خبز
mixer	xallāṭ (m)	خلّاط
coffee machine	mākinat ṣanʿ al qahwa (f)	ماكينة صنع القهوة
kettle	barrād (m)	برّاد
teapot	barrād aʃʃāy (m)	برّاد الشاي
TV set	tilivizyūn (m)	تليفزيون
VCR (video recorder)	ʒihāz tasʒīl vidiyu (m)	جهاز تسجيل فيديو
iron (e.g., steam ~)	makwāt (f)	مكواة
telephone	hātif (m)	هاتف

20052282R00046

Made in the USA
Lexington, KY
02 December 2018